IMAGES OF WAR
SS SPECIALIST UNITS IN COMBAT

RARE PHOTOGRAPHS FROM WARTIME ARCHIVES

IMAGES OF WAR
SS SPECIALIST UNITS IN COMBAT

RARE PHOTOGRAPHS FROM WARTIME ARCHIVES

BOB CARRUTHERS

Pen & Sword
MILITARY

This edition published in 2018 by

Pen & Sword Military
An imprint of
Pen & Sword Books Ltd.
47 Church Street
Barnsley
South Yorkshire
S70 2AS

ISBN: 9781473868489

A CIP catalogue record for this book is available from the British Library.

Printed and bound in England
By CPI Group (UK) Ltd., Croydon, CR0 4YY

Pen & Sword Books Ltd. incorporates the imprints of Pen & Sword Aviation, Pen & Sword Family History, Pen & Sword Maritime, Pen & Sword Military, Pen & Sword Discovery, Pen & Sword Politics, Pen & Sword Atlas, Pen & Sword Archaeology, Wharncliffe Local History, Wharncliffe True Crime, Wharncliffe Transport, Pen & Sword Select, Pen & Sword Military Classics, Leo Cooper, The Praetorian Press, Claymore Press, Remember When, Seaforth Publishing and Frontline Publishing

For a complete list of Pen & Sword titles please contact

PEN & SWORD BOOKS LIMITED
47 Church Street, Barnsley, South Yorkshire, S70 2AS, England
E-mail: enquiries@pen-and-sword.co.uk
Website: www.pen-and-sword.co.uk

INTRODUCTION

Originally formed in 1933 under the command of Sepp Dietrich, the Waffen-SS was created as the armed wing of the Nazi Party's *Schutzstaffel*. The Waffen-SS grew from three regiments to over thirty-eight divisions during World War II, and served alongside the *Heer, Ordnungspolizei* and other security units. During its twelve year existence the Waffen-SS gained a reputation for ferocity, imagination, resilience, and tenacity that was second to none.

The Waffen-SS began as the *SS-Verfügungstruppe* (SS-VT). They bore this name until August 1940, when Hitler gave the SS-VT its new name: the Waffen-SS. Initially, in keeping with the racial policy of Nazi Germany, membership was open only to people of Germanic origin (so-called Aryan ancestry). Later the rules were partially relaxed, and the formation of units composed largely or solely of foreign volunteers and conscripts was authorised. These SS units were predominantly comprised of men from the nations of Nazi-occupied Europe. Despite relaxation of the rules, the Waffen-SS was still based on the racist ideology of Nazism, and ethnic Poles (who were viewed as subhumans) were barred specifically from the formations.

Though the brainchild of Adolf Hitler and Heinrich Himmler, the military father of the Waffen-SS was Paul Hausser. In November 1934, Hausser was transferred to the *SS-Verfügungstruppe* and assigned to the SS officer training school. In 1936, he became the Inspector of the SS-VT; in this role, Hausser was in charge of the troops' military and ideological training, but did not have command authority as the decision on deployment of the troops remained in Himmler's hands. This aligned with Hitler's order of 17 August 1938, which stated these troops were to be 'neither (a part) of the army, nor of the police'.

While many of its formations were specialized the core units were Panzer, Panzergrenadier, and specialized infantry. The premier Waffen-SS divisions were the 1st SS Panzer Division 'Leibstandarte SS Adolf Hitler', the 2nd SS Panzer Division 'Das Reich', the 3rd SS Panzer Division 'Totenkopf', and the 5th SS Panzer Division 'Wiking' (comprised mostly of foreign volunteers from Western Europe and Scandinavia). The 12th SS Panzer Division 'Hitlerjugend' was formed in 1943, with the majority of its men enlisted from the Hitler Youth, alongside senior NCOs and officers from other Waffen-SS divisions. It joined the other divisions as a premier Waffen-SS fighting unit, quickly earning a reputation for ferocity bordering on fanaticism.

In these pages you will find images of the men who kept these Waffen-SS divisions moving forward. Here are the cavalrymen, artillerymen, signallers, engineers, bakers, medics, mountain troops and a host of other specialists who combined to make the Waffen-SS an effective fighting force.

Sepp Dietrich

With the exception of the North African Campaign, the Waffen-SS took part in every major German offensive during World War II. They exhibited a nearly suicidal aggressiveness, combined with innovative tactics. Unlike in the Wehrmacht, the relationship in the Waffen-SS between officers and their men was much less formal; much as is the case in modern special operations units.

The lack of experienced officers during the opening years of the war led to the Waffen-SS taking unnecessarily high risks, with attendant casualties. This trend would continue throughout the war; though from 1942 onward this was less of an issue, as the Waffen-SS divisions gradually became among the most experienced and tactically capable in the German Armed Forces.

When Hitler launched Operation Barbarossa, he expected the Wehrmacht to conquer the Soviet Union and the Waffen-SS to carry out the goals of the party; stating 'We have only to kick in the front door and the whole rotten structure will come tumbling down.'

To the Waffen-SS, therefore, fell not just the job of combat but also waging a race war to create Hitler's long cherished dream of *Lebensraum*, the much anticipated living space for the German people in the East. However, as events spiralled out of control, the war in the East became the most titanic struggle in the history of warfare, with the ever expanding Waffen-SS at the heart of that terrible conflict. During operations in the East, the Waffen-SS grew from just six divisions comprising 160,000 men at the start of Barbarossa until, by the end of the war, it represented a huge force of thirty-eight divisions comprising over 950,000 men.

At the victory parade in Red Square in Moscow on 24 June 1945, pride of place among the captured Nazi standards was reserved for the banner of the 1st SS Panzer Division 'Leibstandarte SS Adolf Hitler'.

The men of the Waffen-SS you see in this volume were the Nazi idealists. They had bought into the Nazi creed of expansion to the East in search of *Lebensraum*. As a highly mobile and modern miniature version of the German army the Waffen-SS needed to develop all of the specialist units that are necessary to keep fighting.

The policy of *Lebensraum* implicitly assumed the superiority of Germans as members of an Aryan master race who by virtue of their heritage had the right to displace people deemed to be part of inferior races. In 1941, it was therefore the stated policy of the Nazis to kill, deport, or enslave Slavic populations, and to repopulate the land with Germanic people drawn primarily from the ranks of the Waffen-SS.

The grand plan was to create an agricultural surplus grown by the new population of warrior farmers who were to be rewarded with grants of land in recognition for their service in the ranks of the Waffen-SS.

The man tasked with giving concrete form to Hitler's vision was Himmler and it was he who controlled the Waffen-SS in practical terms.

Under the command of Himmler, the Waffen-SS received privileged treatment in terms of weapons and supplies. As a consequence they selected only the most committed recruits who were willing to fight and die for the cause. With the advantages that sprang from highly motivated recruits, excellent equipment, cohesive background requirements and an all-embracing ideological indoctrination, the Waffen-SS soon earned a fearsome reputation in combat. This hard won reputation was combined with a fanatical loyalty to Hitler, and encapsulated in the motto 'Meine Ehre heißt Treue' or 'My Honour Is Loyalty'.

Paul 'Papa' Hausser

By the end of 1941, the Waffen-SS had suffered over 43,000 casualties across the length of the Eastern Front. One in four Waffen-SS soldiers had either been killed or wounded.

From 1943 onwards, in order to counter what he interprpeted as the defeatist attitude of the army, Hitler increasingly turned to the Waffen-SS whose loyalty and fighting spirit were never in question. The Wehrmacht's loss became the Waffen-SS's gain as the Führer's 'fire brigade' were used to plug the gaps and hold the line against the advancing Red Army.

As the situation in the East deteriorated conscripts were drawn from an ever more diverse ethnic mix typified by the 13th Waffen Mountain Division of the SS 'Handschar' which was composed of Bosnian Muslims. This unit conducted anti-partisan activities in Yugoslavia and Croatia during 1944. By the finish of World War II nearly half of the Waffen-SS were non-ethnic Germans despite the original strict racial requirements laid down by Himmler.

To the end, Hitler possessed an almost blind faith in the fighting ability of the Waffen-SS. This was despite the fact that many of the later divisions were only regiment or brigade sized units. Furthermore, the ranks were all too often filled by conscripts who lacked the experience and dedication of the original formations. As losses mounted the cadres from the original elite SS divisions were amalgamated to form mechanised Panzer Corps, which soon became the backbone of the German Army.

As the war in the East moved to Poland and eventually Germany, Waffen-SS troops were among the final soldiers defending the ruins of the Reich Chancellery in Berlin. Hitler finally committed suicide on 30 April 1945, and when news of his death reached them, many of the remaining Waffen-SS troops shot themselves rather than surrender.

When hostilities finally ceased on 8 May 1945, nearly one in three Waffen-SS troops were dead or missing in action. For an elite fighting force that never made up more than

Heinrich Himmler

ten per cent of the total German Army and had numbered just 120 men in 1933, they had fought with almost reckless fanaticism and paid a very high price. Their mortality rate was the equivalent of all the casualties suffered by the United States military during the entire war.

Based on the evidence of their combat record the Waffen-SS are often hailed as an elite fighting force. However, while it is true that this force fought exceptionally well in military terms, in social and humanitarian terms the reputation of the Waffen-SS will always be tainted by the war crimes they committed in the East and the West. Praise for the Waffen-SS in the annals of World War II therefore needs to be balanced against their sinister motive and the utter ruthlessness they showed, particularly towards the Jews, Soviets, and later the Poles.

At the post-war Nuremberg trials, the Waffen-SS was judged to be a criminal organisation due to its connection to the Nazi Party and direct involvement in numerous war crimes and crimes against humanity. Accordingly history has judged the Waffen-SS not, as they would have wished, by their combat record but instead far more ignominiously by the atrocities they carried out; a legacy that endures to this day.

Dispatch riders of the Army and the Waffen SS (foreground) direct the forward march of the columns.

Combat engineers of the Waffen-SS receive their orders prior to an attack.

Anti-tank troops accompany the forward units in order to engage enemy armour as required.

Kradschützen Truppen (motorcycle reconnaissance units) press forward on the Western Front.

The men of the reconnaissance units were able to quickly dismount and engage the enemy.

Waffen-SS grenadiers on the march were required to carry as much ammunition as possible.

The 1st SS Panzer Division 'Leibstandarte SS Adolf Hitler' pick up paratroopers from a Junkers 52.

Combat engineers of the 3rd SS Panzer Division 'Totenkopf' build an emergency bridge.

A casualty from the 'Germania' Regiment is transported by a *Kradmelder* (dispatch rider).

A casualty from the 1st SS Panzer Division 'Leibstandarte SS Adolf Hitler' is brought safely into the care of a *Sani* (medical orderly).

A reporter and photographers of the *SS-Kriegsberichter-Kompanie* (SS War Reporter Company).

The Field Bakery Company baked 12,000 loaves every day.

German sausage to go with the bread. A veterinary surgeon checks the quality of the meat.

Infantry of the 3rd SS Panzer Division 'Totenkopf'.

Anti-aircraft defence of the 3rd SS Panzer Division 'Totenkopf' by the Moerdyk bridge.

Waffen-SS comabt engineers prepare to cross a river.

Dispatch rider of the 4th SS 'Polizei' Panzergrenadier Division.

NCO of the 4th SS 'Polizei' Panzergrenadier Division attends to the horse-drawn transport.

A range-finder for the heavy-infantry guns.

Waffen-SS troops storm a beach during a combat training exercise on the Channel coast.

Men of the 3rd SS Panzer Division 'Totenkopf' operating heavy artillery on the coast.

Men of the 3rd SS Panzer Division 'Totenkopf' operating heavy artillery on the Channel coast.

A 7.5 cm leichtes Infanteriegeschütz 18 infantry support gun.

An early version of the Sturmgeschütz (StuG III Ausf.C/D).

In the training area: a Maschinengewehr 34 (MG 34), a recoil-operated air-cooled machine gun.

1941 – A light armoured scout-car stops to observe in the Balkans.

A field medical officer vaccinates fourfold against typhoid fever, paratyphoid fever, cholera and smallpox.

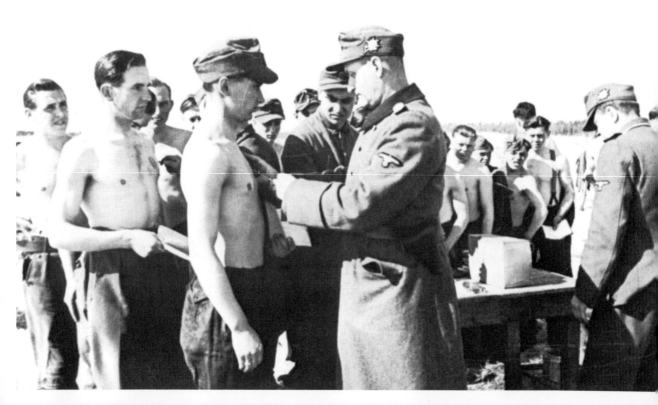

An MG 34 in tripod mode operated by *Kradschützen Truppen*. Motorcycles are seen in the background.

A Serbian prisoner is questioned by the advancing *Kradschützen Truppen*.

Kradschützen Truppen and scout-cars at the forefront of the advance through Greece.

Treacherous conditions make it difficult for four-wheeled vehicles to advance.

Heavy artillery helps the Waffen-SS force the passes. The Klidi Pass was taken on 12 April 1941 and the Klisura Pass was taken on 14 April 1941.

Combat engineers blow up obstacles to open up the way forward.

Waffen-SS troops commandeer Greek sailing vessels on the Isthmus of Corinth in order to rendezvous with their Fallschirmjäger comrades.

1941 – An *Aufklärung* (reconnaissance) battalion of the 5th SS Panzer Division 'Wiking' advance on the Eastern Front.

Kradschützen Truppen of the 2nd SS Panzer Division 'Das Reich' pass through a Russian village.

The machine gunner was the backbone of the Waffen SS infantry fire power.

Motorcycle infantry of the 5th SS Panzer Division 'Wiking' to the south of the Eastern Front.

Dismounted Waffen SS cavalry advance on foot.

Kradschützen Truppen of the 1st SS Panzer Division 'Leibstandarte SS Adolf Hitler' on the attack.

Reconnaissance elements of the 2nd SS Panzer Division 'Das Reich' in a forest near Chominski.

Every day the butchery company turns 55 head of cattle or 120 pigs into fresh meat for the division.

A 7.5 cm leichtes Infanteriegeschütz 18 infantry support gun is brought into action.

A German medic hastily applies a bandage to the head of a wounded comrade on the Eastern Front.

In position with their 3.7 cm Pak 36 anti-tank gun, a Waffen-SS gun crew opens fire on a distant target on the Russian Front in 1941.

A 2 cm anti-aircraft gun is manoeuvred into position.

Dressed in summer camouflage, a Waffen-SS grenadier estimates the range to a target for the artillery using a Entfernungsmesser 34. Billowing skyward in the background is smoke from an earlier direct hit.

Making a telephone connection – the HQ troops had the job of maintaining communications.

Men of the 5th SS Panzer Division 'Wiking' with a flame thrower.

River obstacles were overcome using assault craft and rubber dinghies.

An MG 34 machine-gun, mounted on its tripod, fires on long-range targets. The MG 34 had a rate of fire of 900 rounds per minute and while it was theoretically replaced by MG 42, it remained in wide use with production continuing to the end of the war.

Building roads involved the infantry as well as the engineers.

The MG 42 in action. Its unique sound led to it being nicknamed 'Hitler's buzzsaw'.

An *Aufklärungsabteilung* of the 5th SS Panzer Division 'Wiking' scout ahead of the infantry and tanks. 'Wiking' Division was recruited from Scandinavian, Finnish, Estonian, Dutch, and Belgian volunteers but served under German officers. However, recruitment proved to be sluggish and the bulk of the rank and file were German citizens.

Up in the far north, the 6th SS Mountain Division 'Nord' fought up on the further side of the Arctic Circle, deep in the woods and among the marshes and lakes of Karelia.

1941 – A heavy machine-gun in the forest on the road to Louhi, covering the Murmansk railway.

Reconnaissance troops are always in the field to prevent the enemy springing any surprises and to prepare the way for their own sides' operations.

Waffen-SS troops with an MG 34. The legs could be extended to allow to be used as an anti-aircraft gun or lowered so it could be used as an infantry support weapon.

White winter overcoats were issued to advancing troops. Frostbite took a terrible toll and many troops lost limbs or were deemed unfit to fight.

An anti-tank gun gives cover.

Elements of the 8th SS Cavalry Division 'Florian Geyer' advance.

Food supplies are transported forward in Thermos containers.

Waffen-SS combat engineers construct a bridge.

Waffen-SS horses drink from a pond during a period of rest.

A field blacksmith.

The 4th Squadron of the 2nd SS Mounted Regiment.

A break at midday for the sqaudron.

A heavy field howitzer being operated in battle.

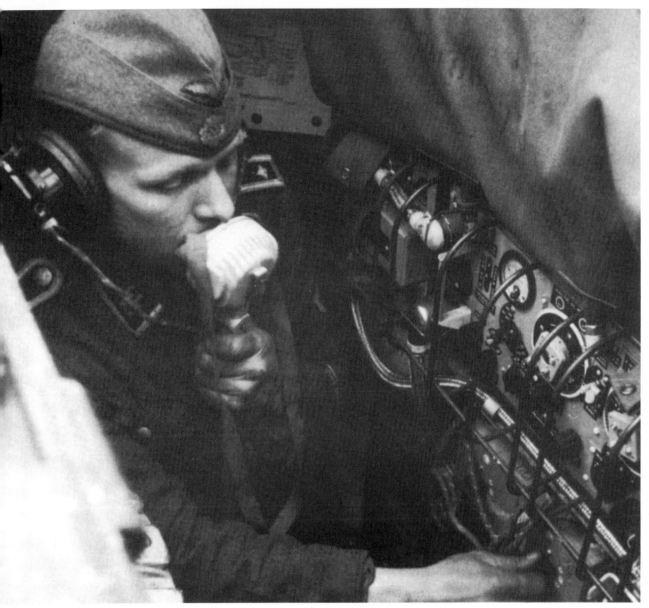

Radio and telephone operators are indispensable to those in command.

Observation on all sides from an armoured car.

A reconnaissance patrol in action.

A 7.5 cm anti-tank gun (Pak 40) with 22 hits to its credit.

A 3.7 cm anti-aircraft gun protects a bridge.

A light 2 cm anti-aircraft gun on a self-propelled gun carriage.

An amphibious vehicle – the propeller is engaged.

An armoured scout car of the 1st SS Panzer Division 'Leibstandarte SS Adolf Hitler'.

Building an emergency bridge, protected by the Waffen-SS anti-aircraft artillery.

Observers – they see but they are not seen.

Doctors of both the Waffen SS and the Army in a joint visit to a field hospital. Lines of ambulances transport the wounded away, whilst more serious cases are transported back in a Fieseler 'Stork'.

The medical equipment is checked over.

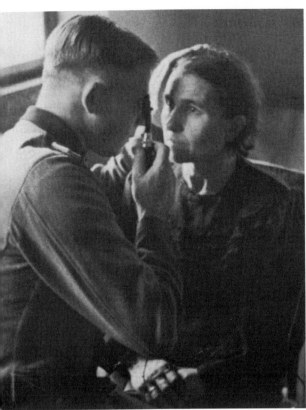
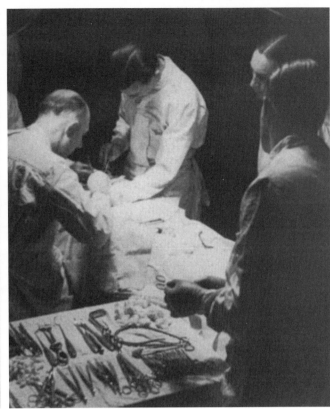

(Left) SS-Hauptsturmführer Dr. Buchsteiner, an army doctor (killed in action), attends to a Russian civilian. (Right) Surgeons performing their difficult work in the field hospital of a medical company.

(Left) A 'Sani' (medical orderly) offers first-aid to a wounded soldier. (Right) A young army doctor..

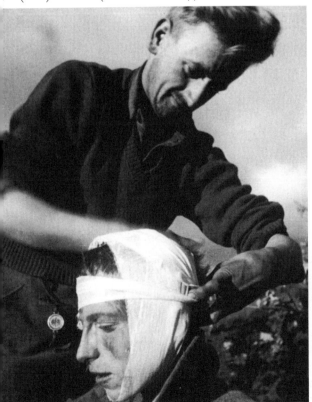

A Volkswagen Schwimmwagen of the 1st SS Panzer Division 'Leibstandarte SS Adolf Hitler'.

A joint Waffen SS and Army reconnaissance.

An infantry field gun under a camouflage net.

Motorcycle infantry of the 27th SS Volunteer Division 'Langemarck'.

Waffen-SS soldiers work together to free a motorcycle from the mud as they ready to attack.

Waffen SS and Army soldiers together rescue a badly wounded soldier.

A grenadier from the 8th SS Cavalry Division 'Florian Geyer' holds a Tellermine 43 anti-tank blast mine. Between March 1943 and the end of World War II, over 3.6 million Tellermine 43s were produced by Germany. Packed with 5.5 kilograms of TNT and with a detonation pressure of about 200 pounds, it was capable of blowing the tracks off any Soviet tank.

Heavy artillery on the march.

All arms carried a weight of expectation – mortars...

heavy machine-guns...

and radio transmitters...

but the main burden lies with the infantry.

A 7.5 cm anti-tank gun in position...

well camouflaged and defensively covered.

A reconnaissance patrol in a sunflower field.

(Left) Supplies are transported to the front. (Right) The forward observer with a scissors periscope.

July 1943 – A Waffen-SS machine-gunner during the second Battle of Kursk.

Waffen-SS infantry put the MG 34 to use on the Eastern Front.

This four-barrelled 2 cm anti-aircraft gun is always ready to fire during the railway journey.

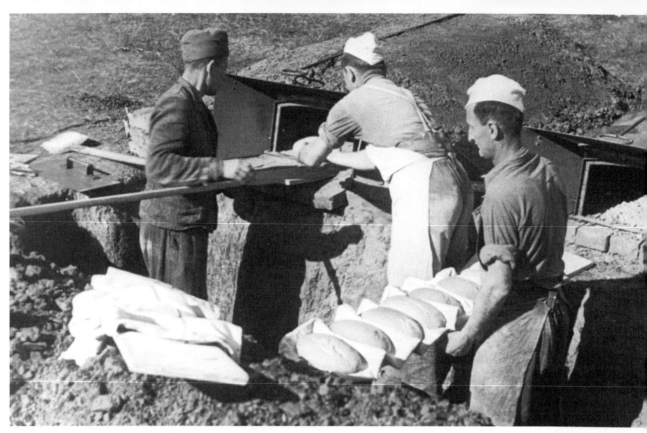

Field bakery ovens of the 7th SS Volunteer Mountain Division 'Prinz Eugen' and mobile field bakery ovens of the 9th SS Panzer Division 'Hohenstaufen'. A loaf made of 750 grams of rye flour and called *Kommißbrot* was the staple food and was made by the troops' own bakery companies.

Waffen-SS signal troops move into position.

Waffen-SS signallers fix up a telephone line and check to see that it is in working order.

A medium anti-aircraft gun of the 2nd SS Panzer Division 'Das Reich' at Byelgorod.

1943 – An officer of the 8th SS Cavalry Division 'Florian Geyer' takes a short break to eat a meal. These men were used in anti-partisan actions in 1943.

Artillery at Belly-Kdodesi.

A mobile anti-tank gun and snipers at Losovaya.

Wrecked vehicles of the 1st SS Panzer Division 'Leibstandarte SS Adolf Hitler' in the Kegitshevka area.

20 February 1943 – A Russian anti-tank gun has been knocked out, Kasatchi-Maidan.

The harsh winter conditions set limits to the swift *Kradschützen Truppen* of the 2nd SS Panzer Division 'Das Reich'.

A light field gun being transported in a snow storm.

The same gun in action at Yeremeyevka.

River crossings were quickly accomplished with the aid of special bridging equipment.

Kradschützen Truppen of the 7th SS Volunteer Mountain Division 'Prinz Eugen' push forward.

Waffen-SS soldiers manning a Czechoslovak ZB-53 machine-gun on its tripod, east of Ripac.

Waffen-SS mountain troops utilise all available local resources.

Artillery and mountain troops of the 7th SS Volunteer Mountain Division 'Prinz Eugen'.

Troops of the 7th SS Volunteer Mountain Division 'Prinz Eugen' use their forage-caps to drink from a mountain spring.

Reconnaissance troops of the 7th SS Volunteer Mountain Division 'Prinz Eugen' enter Mostar.

A mountain gun puts enemy emplacements out of action.

Exhausted mountain troops use a short break to get some much needed sleep.

Kradschützen Truppen advancing on Lukovo in Montenegro.

At Livin, a donkey carries a load for a mountain trooper who is also carrying a load on his shoulders.

Pack animals were an invaluable asset to the mountain troops of the Waffen-SS.

A short rest on the top of the pass.

A gun maintenance workshop and a de-lousing centre. Both are just as important in the maintenance of the troops' fitness.

The final actions in Operation Schwarz lead through territory which offers the defenders many advantages because of its character.

Marching to Stoca.

Morning mist hangs over the valley.

Transport of the wounded is especially difficult here.

Up in the highlands near Grozd in Montenegro, the mountain infantry exploit every bit of cover.

A steep pass near Tušinja.

Down to the valley on the shoulders of their comrades.

The customary means of towing in the country.

Mountain troops must take everything with them that they need to survive.

The attack starts.

1943 – Men of the 7th SS Volunteer Mountain Division 'Prinz Eugen' help each other in climbing a mountain rock in the Dinaric Alps, Croatia.

The long march: Kupa – Slunj – Bihac – Vrtoce – Petrovac – Grahovo – Livno – Lise – Mostar – Nevesinje – Gacko – Bileca – Nikšić – Gvozd – Savnik.

A 4 barrelled anti-aircraft gun manned by volunteer soldiers from Bosnia and Herzegovina.

The forward observer.

Anti-tank troops in position.

Companies of amphibious vehicles ready to advance.

The training school of the Waffen SS mountain troops in Neustift in the Stubai valley.

Signals practice up in the mountains.

Instruction outdoors.

Teaching the lie of the land.

Mountain infantry sketching the lie of the land.

A training course at the school for mountain troops.

A reconnaissance patrol in their snow coveralls.

Men of the 8th SS Cavalry Division 'Florian Geyer'.

1944 – Waffen-SS Latvian volunteers in action on the Eastern Front. Here a sniper and his spotter go in for the kill.

A Waffen-SS sniper assesses his target with his field glasses.

Combat engineers erecting supports during the construction of a bridge and transporting troops across a river by towing them on a ferry.

Motorcycle tractors with cross-country capability.

The wounded leader of a reconnaissance group briefs his successor.

The medical officer cannot always save a life.

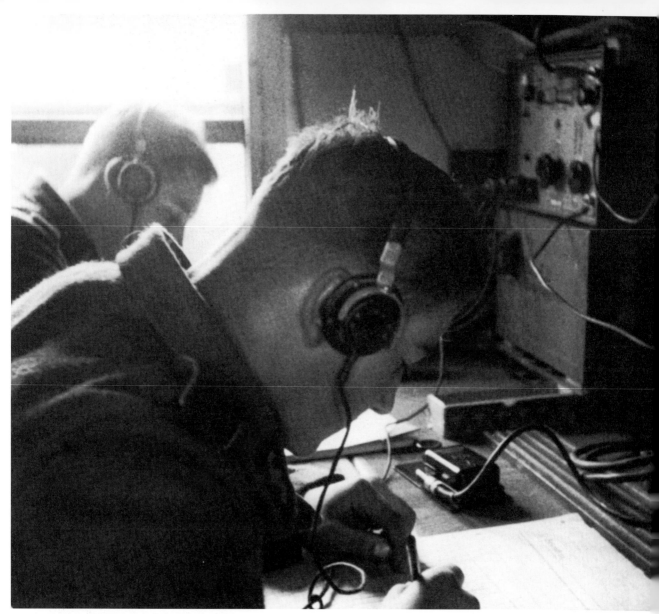

Radio operators decode messages....

... and fill their cartridge belts.

An alert at Volchov for the 4th SS 'Polizei' Panzergrenadier Division.

The famous 8.8 cm anti-aircraft gun shooting at ground targets.

Radio operators of the 2nd SS Panzer Division 'Das Reich' near Kolomak.

Heavy infantry weapons are brought into position.

Radio operators listen in to everything and often know more than anyone else.

Anti-tank troops of the 2nd SS Panzer Division 'Das Reich' at Okhotshaya.

Early 1944 – Officers of the 7th SS Volunteer Mountain Division 'Prinz Eugen' inspect the dead body of a partisan who was shot by a sniper in Osoje, Croatia.

A Waffen-SS signaller checks for interference.

1944 – These soldiers of the 7th SS Volunteer Mountain Division 'Prinz Eugen' were shot at by partisans in a village on the Balkan peninsula and are returning fire.

The 2 cm four barrelled anti-tank gun was highly effective against both ground and airborne targets.

A soldier of 7th SS Volunteer Mountain Division 'Prinz Eugen' surveys the area with his field glasses.

27 April 1944 – Combat engineers of the 5th SS Panzer Division 'Wiking' work to repair a collapsing railroad bed, roughly 4 kilometres southwest of Kovel. The tracks gave way under the weight of SS-Obersturmbannführer Otto Paetsch's command tank.

25 May 1944 – Paratroopers of the SS-Fallschirmjägerbataillon 500 collect their thoughts on the approach to the Bosnian town of Drvar during the beginning of Operation Rösselsprung. The SS-Fallschirmjägerbataillon 500 was a Waffen-SS special ops forces unit and this was their first airborne raid and would be conducted deep into the heart of enemy territory, on the communist partisan headquarters with the aim to kill or capture the communist partisan leader Josip Broz Tito.

Army and Waffen-SS troops under the command of General Rendulic and supported by strong bomber and ground-attack aircraft formations, attacked the headquarters of Tito's guerilla groups and smashed it after several days of fighting. In the fighting, the 7th SS Volunteer Mountain Division 'Prinz Eugen' under the command of SS-Oberführer Kumm and the SS-Fallschirmjägerbataillon 500 under the command of SS-Hauptsturmführer Rybka, gave excellent service.

(Left) Heinkel bombers dropping the paratroops and (right) a ground attack aircraft tows a glider.

25 May 1944 – Members of the SS-Fallschirmjägerbataillon 500 carrying a supply container in Drvar.

The SS-Fallschirmjäger's signals position.

An SS-Fallschirmjäger commander with Air Force officers.

25 May 1944 – A glider team from the SS-Fallschirmjägerbataillon 500 clears its aircraft after landing at Drvar at the start of Operation Rösselsprung.

A paratrooper of the SS-Fallschirmjägerbataillon 500 in the town of Drvar, during Operation Rösselsprung. The operation was bound to be highly dangerous because the paratroopers had intrinsic weaknesses: stocks of supplies – ammunition, food and water – were low; once dropped their mobility was limited; heavy fire support could only be provided by air power; and in the event of failure a relieving ground force rather than withdrawal was the only hope of survival.

Men of the SS-Fallschirmjägerbataillon 500 in position. The NCO in the foreground carries an MP 40 submachine gun in his right hand and a spare MG barrel case over his left shoulder.

A parachuted weapon container in the front line.

SS-Fallschirmjägerbataillon 500 radio operators. They provided contact with the Higher Command and the advancing ground force, as well as coordinating needed air support with Luftwaffe.

The attack on Tito's headquarters begins.

Men of the SS-Fallschirmjägerbataillon 500 wearing camouflage uniforms in Kraljevo, Serbia. The soldier on the far right looks equipped with a ammunition bag for an MP 40.

June 1944 – Paratroopers of the SS-Fallschirmjägerbataillon 500 during Operation Rösselsprung.

SS-Fallschirmjäger mortar crew in action.

The paratroopers' main dressing station.

July 1944 – SS-Fallschirmjägerbataillon 500 during the Vilnius Offensive. Vilnius is the capital of Lithuania, and the site of the siege by Soviet troops after the launching of the offensive which took place on 5-13 July, 1944. Many of the units of the Wehrmacht and Waffen-SS were trapped in a pocket which was later renamed by the Germans as a Fester Platz (Fortress), and among them was the SS-Fallschirmjägerbataillon 500.

29 July 1944 – Men of the SS-Fallschirmjägerbataillon 500 near the river Neman, in the city of Kaunas in Lithuania. This photograph was taken shortly after the conclusion of Operation Rösselsprung.

Anti-tank troops of the 29th Waffen Grenadier Division of the SS (1st Italian).

A Dutch volunteer handling a clipbelt, full of ammunition.

1944 – Meeting of the command of the SS-Fallschirmjägerbataillon 600.

Latvian volunteers wade through a small river.

Soldiers of the 28th SS Volunteer Grenadier Division 'Wallonien' with a medium mortar.

Volunteers of the 20th Waffen Grenadier Division of the SS (1st Estonian) in the East.

Men of the 20th Waffen Grenadier Division of the SS (1st Estonian) attempt a river crossing on a makeshift raft.

A soldier of the 27th SS Volunteer Division 'Langemarck' with an MG 34 machine-gun mounted on a Lafette 34 tripod.

1944 – Danish volunteers during the Battle of Narva, in Estonia. One man is seen sleeping whilst another mans a machine-gun.

Teller mines were laid according to a plan, so that they could be collected again if neccessary.

An examination by the military doctor is scrupulously carried out. (French volunteers being examined).

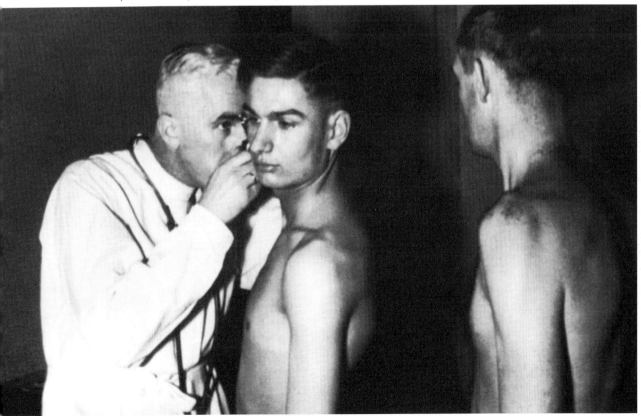

An officer indicates targets to Hungarian vounteers of the Waffen-SS. They are seen alongside a 20 mm anti-aircraft gun.

Young French volunteers of the Waffen-SS with an MG 42 machine-gun.

1944 – The 3rd Battery of the Flak battalion of the 11th SS Volunteer Panzergrenadier Division 'Nordland' at the Narva bridgehead.

A Dutch volunteer brings up some barbed wire to build an obstacle in the River Narva area.

Panzerschreck was the popular name for the *Raketenpanzerbüchse*, an 88 mm calibre reusable anti-tank rocket launcher. Another popular nickname was *Ofenrohr* ('stove pipe').

10 June 1944 – An aid post of the Fallschirmjäger and the 17th SS Panzergrenadier Division 'Götz von Berlichingen' near Carentan.

A sniper of the 6th SS Mountain Division 'Nord'.

Dispatch riders – indispensable to the command of a motorized unit.

An anti-tank gun in the Karelian forests east of Kietinki. Soldiers with anti-fly veils.